D1610997

'We are the music-makers
And we are the
dreamers of dreams'
Arthur O'Shaughnessy,
via Willy Wonka

Time After Time

Minna Gilligan

hardie grant books

Contents

Introduction

INTRODUCTION

I think the first such instance in which I recall being infatuated with a piece of clothing was when I was four years old. My sisters and I had a dress-up box: a rather old, army-green canvas and leather chest that housed various garments and accessories my Nanna and mother had scrounged together for us. The majority of the items were, I would estimate, circa 1970s and 1980s — lots of chiffon, sequins and tulle. There were also my Nanna's very petite gloves from the 1950s and 1960s, in pastel shades with little intricate embroidery details, the pairs of which we could never find. My favourite dress-up box find was an elaborate emerald green dress that actually deserves to be described as a gown.

It was the archetypal dress-up-box dress. Altogether too big for me, I'd get around tripping up on the hem and not minding because I was so besotted with the glamour it contributed to an otherwise rather regular afternoon in the Gilligan household. This is when I first became aware of the power a garment could give to its wearer. The power to control circumstances, enhance narratives, excite onlookers and elevate the wearer to whoever he or she longed to be.

Playing dress ups as a child isn't an unusual vocation, but that exploratory, mish-mash and 'anything goes' way of dressing is something I never actually grew out of. It still took me a little while to gravitate to thrift shopping. In the throes of a few teenage obsessions with perhaps atypical subjects—principally the likes of Edie Sedgwick and Madonna—I began to feel strongly about this idea of identity: particularly, forging an identity through ways of dressing. Edie Sedgwick in the sixties—signature black leggings, stripey tops and chandelieresque earrings—and Madonna in the eighties—torn stockings, stacks of rubber bracelets, high-waisted 'mom' jeans and rags tied in her hair as bows—were major inspirations of mine. They wielded such fabulous power by having a 'look', and it became my mission to find my own.

I started my search tentatively at the local Savers, a giant thrift store just a short train ride from my house. I'd passed it many a time, never really giving it a lot of thought as being somewhere tremendously exciting. As I walked hesitantly through those wonky sliding doors for the first time, believe you me, I was like Veruca Salt walking into Willy Wonka's chocolate factory. The first items I bought were sort of obnoxiously eighties printed silk scarves. I had this idea to cut the middle out of them and make them into some sort of swing top. While I am not very good at sewing, I managed to somehow fashion it using a couple of safety pins and a sewing machine to make a pitiful, wonky hem.

INTRODUCTION

I wore this rather sculptural creation out to dinner with my family and a woman approached me and complimented me on it. I was hooked.

I wonder if I'd even be writing this book had I not grown up in such close proximity to that Savers store; what I'd be doing with my life had I not had that out-of-the-blue notion to walk inside. I returned the next week, and the next, and the week after that: it quickly became my haven.

Concocting outfits as a teenager was truly my greatest devotion. It provided the highest form of escapism short of actually leaving my room. Despite being an (at times) tortured introvert, the idea that I could convey ideas, assume characters and act out narratives through my outfits was an integral form of expression that didn't necessarily mean I had to be an extrovert. As soon as I discovered it, there was no looking back: dressing in particular ways allowed me to be the protagonist I'd always wanted to be.

My interest in bygone eras, I believe, stems from a desire to slow down the dizzying present. My memories, dreams and fantasies are infinitely more attractive than the gritty 'now'. The reason I'm infatuated with notions of the past is because I can curate and mould them into my wildest fantasies, the ultimate realms to escape within; so brilliant they cannot exist in real life. My fantasies are cinematic, technicolour, misty and ultimately unreal. My outfits allow me to both create these worlds and exist within them. They are overarchingly nostalgic in that they reference the inexplicably familiar, and yet are not actually placeable within a particular time or space.

Since this hobby–turned–obsession–turned–lifeblood began, I've collected a huge array of dresses, skirts, tops, accessories and shoes from many sources. My Savers obsession grew to encompass op shops (thrift stores),

vintage and retro stores, eBay, Etsy, flea markets and other moth-infested, allergy-inducing outlets that have the potential to give me the thrill of an incredible find.

As an exceptionally broke teenager I was able to create interesting outfits on a shoestring budget of a few dollars, as well as avoiding the disposable fashion trends that dominated the market for those my age; but even now that I've graduated from university and have a reasonably regular income, I still shop at Savers.

I am also able to occasionally afford the more contemporary high-end items I covet. I love labels such as Romance Was Born, Opening Ceremony, Kenzo, and Tsumori Chisato, to name a few. Thus the idea for this book was born. Combining items from contemporary ranges with retro finds is endlessly fascinating: hybrid looks that encompass several decades and demonstrate the ease with which you can merge seemingly unrelated, unmatching items into the outfits of your wildest dreams. I want to help you identify your personal aesthetic, the look you want to convey, the person you want to be, if only for a day.

My aesthetic is overwhelmingly colourful and playful. I put together outfits the way I make collage artworks; seaming together various elements plucked from different time periods into one cohesive, yet still interesting, entity.

The luxury of living in the age of the internet is that, ultimately, we have access to a time machine. We can appropriate looks and ideas we come across in late-night YouTube or Tumblr trawls. It seems everything is up for grabs, everything is in reach. Not only are we able to directly take inspiration from these sources, but we are able to look back and change things we believe to be unsuccessful. Being able to look at things in retrospect is the greatest of luxuries. We can curate our past and our present.

Op Shopping Advice

Op Shopping Advice

Over the years, I've had a number of different strategies for op shops (thrift stores). They have developed somewhat in sophistication and intricacy but none require a particularly large amount of skill, technique or brainpower: just a bit of practice.

First and foremost, I want to stress that I don't see op shopping as a kind of business or money-making venture. I'm not scouring for specific labels or super bargains that I can sell on for profit. I don't believe op shopping should be like that, really: I think it's about luck and chance and only buying things you truly feel an affinity with, not choosing them because they may be 'valuable'. If I'm op shopping, it's purely for my own wardrobe and enjoyment, not to make money.

AMERICA STANDS UNITED

What follows is my own comprehensive list of things you need to get started.

Time

The number one thing you must have when op shopping is time. If you have to rush around the store without paying proper attention to things, there is every chance you will miss out on a really great find. You don't want to be in a hurry: you need to be feeling relaxed and in a calm state of mind to be searching through things, so you're able to see the true potential of each item you come across.

Optimism

You have to be optimistic. Fortunately I've been blessed with a daftly hopeful disposition and tend to walk into op shops with a sparkling feeling that I'm going to find something wonderful. Usually, this premonition comes true, and I'm very grateful for this. If, by chance, I leave a store empty handed, that's okay too, because I know that next time I try, I'm even more likely to find something great.

Op Shopping Advice

Patience

If you don't have near-saintly patience, op shopping isn't going to be for you. It involves oh-so-carefully rifling through rack after rack, considering every item you come across, vigilant not to miss anything. It's not a quick or brash process. Be methodical and calculating. No stone must be left unturned!

A good eye

Do you know what you like? Good. Op shopping is a thousand times easier if you have an aesthetic you enjoy. That way, you know when you've found something brilliant that you'll get use from. My aesthetic, for example, is colourful, playful and psychedelic. This means that I am pretty into clothing and objects from the 1960s and 1970s. I know that sixties and seventies clothes are most likely to be polyester, and usually in really dynamic colours with floral or linear patterns. This makes the whole process go a little quicker because I have a vague idea in my mind what it is I'm searching for.

21

Op Shopping Advice

I have purchased a number of items that have led to my sanity being questioned, mostly by my mum. Okay, so sometimes I don't get it right and I buy something that is a little too strange or shoulder-padded to pull off. In that case it goes right back to the op shop; however, most of the time I do get it right. Trust yourself and your judgment. If you see something that looks pretty wild on the hanger but seems too good to pass up, imagine it in rotation in your wardrobe, paired with items you already have. If you can (sometimes op shops don't have change rooms) try it on and get a feel for how you could wear it. More often than not, if you love it, it will work, no matter how big those shoulder pads are. If not, it was only a couple of dollars. There's no shame in buying the occasional thing and getting it home only to realise how wrong you were. Just donate it back to the op shop and try again.

Be a lone wolf: op shopping is best done alone. You have to focus on the task at hand and minimise all possible distractions. If you don't want to go alone, go with someone like a parent or sibling. If I am to go with someone, I will go with my mum on a Sunday or Monday morning, when it's quiet. We 'split up' once we arrive, only occasionally checking in with each other to see what we've both found. This works well. An op shopping partner must have the same ambition and drive as you do otherwise they will ONLY BRING YOU DOWN.

Choosiness

Be very, very picky. I do not buy items that smell or are damaged, stained and torn. I also avoid buying items that need to be majorly altered to fit me, as I know that it's rare that I will get around to it!

Putting Outfits Together

Putting Outfits Together

Putting an outfit together
can initially seem to be a daunting task.
When I was younger, a number of thoughts
would go through my mind...

My top six high-school-brain thoughts:

1• Is this outfit 'cool'?

2• Will this outfit gain the approval of my friends and peers?

3• Does this outfit make me look 'good' and 'hot' in a traditional sense, and yet doesn't make me stand out of the crowd in any intense way?

4• Have I worn this outfit too many times?

5• Does it look like my mum bought me these clothes?

6• Is that a stain?

And then a few last-minute seemingly unimportant thoughts:

1• Will I be warm enough in this?

2• Am I comfortable? Are these shoes going to give me horrific blisters?

3• Oh yeah, does this outfit make ME feel confident and good about myself?

Regency
ALPHABET
BISCUITS
85g NET

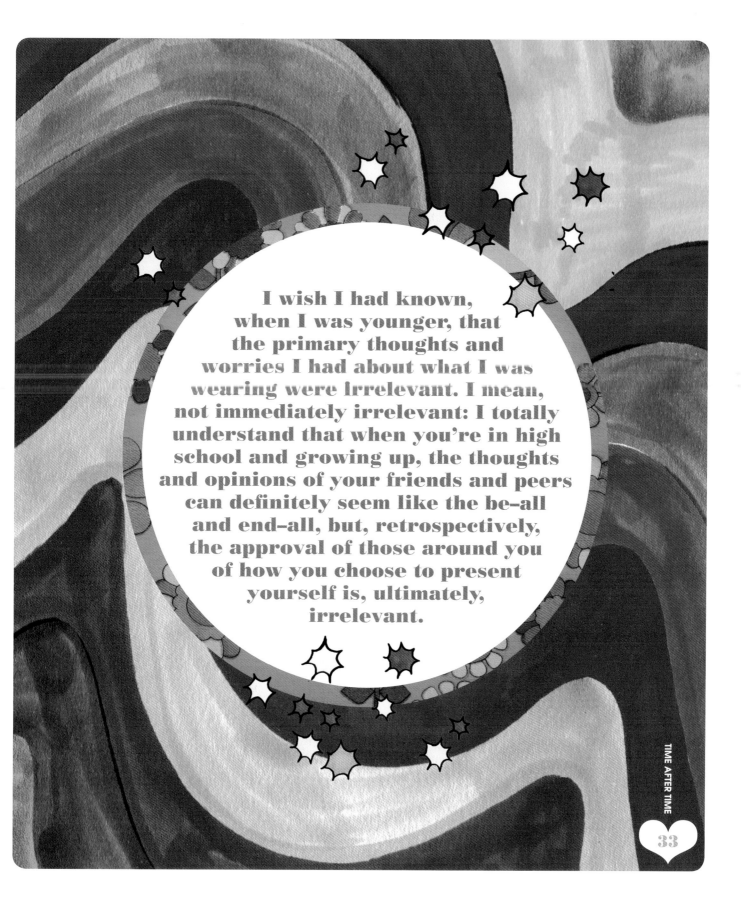

I wish I had known, when I was younger, that the primary thoughts and worries I had about what I was wearing were irrelevant. I mean, not immediately irrelevant: I totally understand that when you're in high school and growing up, the thoughts and opinions of your friends and peers can definitely seem like the be–all and end–all, but, retrospectively, the approval of those around you of how you choose to present yourself is, ultimately, irrelevant.

Putting Outfits Together

Let me explain.

As a relatively shy and reclusive teenager (actually, come think of it, I'm still pretty shy and definitely reclusive), dressing, for me, was about slotting in.

If I wore something that drew attention to myself or that was different from the norm, I was afraid that I would have to be assertive, confident and outspoken in justifying this choice.

This went against my anxiety-driven wallflower tendencies, and the fear of standing out forced me into making safe aesthetic decisions.

Unfortunately for my red hair and me, even at the time when I was convinced I was blending in, this probably wasn't the case...

...as you can spot my locks from a mile away; but I digress. So I tried to blend in anyway. Despite mildly succeeding, I felt unhappy.

It was the kind of unhappiness that you can't pin on anything in particular. Just a feeling of emptiness, of dissatisfaction, of a listless boredom.

Because verbal communication wasn't particularly my forte, and back then I hadn't quite discovered writing, I felt I was without an outlet. Art was great but, at the time, so private.

If you lack confidence, physically and emotionally, showing people your nowhere-near-perfect artwork can be frighteningly traumatic.

Putting Outfits Together

DREAM

The reason I felt unhappy was because I was invested in the thoughts and approval of other people; thus, the person I felt I really was—or at least was becoming—was quashed and distorted. Eventually, as I got a little older, I realised that whatever other people think is completely and totally out of my control; and acting, speaking and dressing in order to meet these invisible constraints is a pointless and exhausting exercise.

After this epiphany of sorts, I had the drive and conviction to have my first experience thrift shopping (explained in detail in the introduction): buying items from different stores not generally accepted by my peers and wearing my concocted outfits without fear of being questioned or put on the spot. If this did occur, I'd simply say that I was wearing what I liked and felt comfortable in: I don't dress for other people, I dress for myself.

At this time, putting an outfit together became not a worrying imposition but something I would look forward to and plan very much in advance. I didn't have enough birthday parties to attend to wear all the outfits I thought up! Now, roughly eight years later, I have updated and simplified my thoughts about putting an outfit together:

1• Do I think this outfit is cool?

2• Do I feel confident, beautiful and powerful in what I am wearing?

If the answer to these two questions is 'Yes', you're good to go.

When the whole thing is simplified, you can have so much fun getting dressed. You can embody different characters and moods. Dressing can be cinematic, outfits can be iconic, styles can become signatures. Once you've gained the confidence to curate outfits entirely of your own accord—independent from the thoughts of anyone but yourself—you can be happy being you on the outside as well as the inside.

Inspiration for Dressing

INSPIRATION FOR DRESSING

I have a vast collection of printed ephemera. Found photographs, old pamphlets, swap cards, letters, postcards, stationery sets, wrapping paper, stickers, books and magazines. When I say 'vast', I mean that there are, like, stacks of books in my room as tall as me, and my bookshelf has a very suspicious-looking lean to it from being arranged so precariously. I used to collect magazine cut-outs as a child, and I suppose it just snowballed from there. My family remains quite concerned but I just tell them that it's all for the GREATER GOOD: my art practice.

Not only for my art practice, though. My collection of imagery is a constant source of inspiration for the way I dress. The walls of my room and studio are plastered with images of characters, patterns and landscapes, from all of which I am able to draw for inclusion in my various creative endeavours. However, inspiration doesn't have to be as black-and-white as seeing an image and then attempting to directly insert an element of that into what you're producing. For me, it's more about being able to read a particular atmosphere in something—in a book, a picture, an object or an encounter—and it is that essence you want to capture and re-embody in what you're creating. I've recreated my picture-plastered walls within the pages of this book, with hope of passing on some inspiration from my cherished collection.

People often ask me, 'Where and how do you get your inspiration?' and I feel like answering with something along these lines: You don't go out to a store and 'get' inspiration. It is a fluid and surprising substance that comes to you in odd and often immaterial ways. Inspiration is EVERYWHERE if you switch your eyes over to looking for it. Inspiration comes to those who are observant and inquisitive. It's in the air, in cinematic vignettes you catch while looking out the window of a train, in unexpected eye contact, in a scent, in an embrace or in a melody. It's also in these miscellaneous images I collect. Photographs are our earthly attempts at solidly capturing those more elusive moments that pass us by frustratingly fleetingly. I hope these pages are around for a while and provide you with some sparks to work with.

MOOD BOARD

JUN 64

MOOD BOARD

CASINO

ABCD

MOOD BOARD

Best Western

SINCERE GREETINGS

Love of Friends
afar and
near

Be your
"Birthday Gifts"
this year.

MOOD BOARD

Spring

Happy Birthday!

MOOD BOARD

PRINCESS tina ANNUAL

MOOD BOARD

JAN · 72

MEMORY'S MIRROR

When thro' this little mirror
You are taking retrospections
I hope you'll find,
It bring to mind,
The happiest REFLECTIONS.

MOOD BOARD

What is love?

LOVE IS LIKE
THE
MEASLES
WE ALL
HAVE TO GO THROUGH IT. Jerome

CHILDREN

WEDNESDAY   PUGSLEY

TAKES GOMEZ CARD

ROCK 'N' ROLL

MOOD BOARD

A happy
New Year.

THE HOLBEIN AVENUE, WILTON PARK.

MOOD BOARD

I'm not afraid of the Big Bad Wolf!! '79

MOOD BOARD

Pensez à moi!

"WHY MUZZLE ME?"

KE UP, PUSSY."

Je Lui
Confie mon
DéSiR

JUL · 60

POSTES

5c

MOOD BOARD

Pioneers Cabin - California Big Trees   130

VI. Qik été abandonné... Berthe

ROSALIND MARQUIS

Fashion Editorial

Fashion Editorial

If you're anything like me, you'll find that particular outfits or clothing combinations evoke certain memories of events that occurred or the circumstances while you were wearing them. At times, what I was wearing for a poignant moment or event is as important and intrinsically linked as any record of what actually happened while I was there. You remember the texture of a raw silk skirt as you rubbed it between your nervous fingers; a slippery strappy top you kept having to adjust awkwardly while you stood on stage; or a sequined cardigan that kept catching on everything.

Outfits and clothing have that skin-to-fabric physicality that make them memorable components of an event; but of course they also have the capacity to provide an outlet for many types of creativity.

Dressing gives you the ability to disguise, to embody a character of your choice or a period in time, to be loud or quiet without saying a word. As soon as I was allowed the freedom to choose what I adorned myself with, I felt as though I had a particular kind of agency over who I was and who I could be. I could control the way I was perceived by the outside world. I could control how I perceived myself. I was the protagonist in my own narrative: it was erratic and unpredictable in theme, but it was *entirely* my own.

Now that I am a bit older, I actually see dressing more as a form of collage. It enables me to reference ideas, memories, characters or time periods and, from these references, to create entirely new hybrid concoctions. The joy and excitement I experience when deciding what to wear will never fade, and I will forever be challenged and stimulated by these choices.

In the pages that follow, I've put together a number of outfits from my wardrobe. Entirely from my personal wardrobe. I want to specify that none of these items of clothing have been gifted to me in exchange for them being featured in this book: all of them were bought with my own hard-earned money and are in here because I truly treasure each and every one of them. The outfits are based on a number of things— characters from films, imagined vignettes, childhood memories, melodies, lyrics, words, family, boyfriends, girlfriends, moments of sadness and, of course, moments of triumph. They are made up of both vintage and contemporary pieces, in 'collages', if you will. These outfits have been born from the experience of being alive *now*, with the luxury of having years of retrospect on the twentieth century, in combination with the increasing accessibility of modern-day avant-garde designers and labels.

I hope you enjoy what I've put together.

ABC

I was never very good at my 123s... but I could do my ABCs. Even though I didn't have much trouble with most of the actual school work, at times, high school was difficult for me.

While I was skilled at not drawing attention to myself, this behaviour felt at odds with the person I ultimately wanted to be. I mean, most art isn't about 'drawing attention to yourself', but the self is intrinsically tied to the work you make and put on display for all to see, and I didn't have the confidence as a teenager to put myself out there in such a big way. In high school I was deeply unsatisfied and searching for something else. I was constantly at odds: wanting to feel comfortable and safe in expressing myself, but also not wanting to do anything to 'rock the boat', thus giving my peers the opportunity to tear me down.

Gradually I gained the confidence I needed to stand by my work. I found what I was looking for when I started art school, and left most of my insecurities from high school coughing in my dust. Early on, what helped me monumentally was playing with the way I dressed. I went to a high school that was strict with uniforms, but at any opportunity we had to wear our own clothing, or when hanging out with friends on the weekend, I had begun to get really experimental with what I'd wear.

This outfit is for you to wear to some lousy out-of-hours school event that you didn't want to go to, like a charity fête or something. You want to show up in a wild outfit that demands attention. Dressing creatively allows you to express so many pent up things despite being shy and socially anxious. Outfits start conversations for you, give you something to talk about, and make everyone aware of your tastes and interests.

Colour Palette

Yellow, dark blue, red, purple

1 • 1970s yellow, blue and maroon check dress
2 • Peter Jensen wedge platform shoes
3 • Romance Was Born crochet-print leggings

THiNK HAPPY

Baby, you and me girl

adventures in paradise

I am a big fan of the singer Minnie Riperton. 'Lovin' You' was her biggest hit, which you'd probably know: it's an eerily high-pitched yet touching declaration of love for a partner.

The album of hers by which I am most captivated is *Adventures in Paradise* (1975). The cover is what does it for me: the richness of the blue juxtaposed with the brown, orange and earthy tones of the foreground. Oh-so-seventies Gypsophila flowers in her hair just tip it over the edge and THEN you see the LION.

I have the utmost admiration for Minnie as a singer, but also as a woman of strength and determination. At only 31, she died of breast cancer. Too young for anyone to pass away, let alone someone so brilliantly talented who still had so many songs in her heart to sing.

This outfit is for meeting someone unexpectedly in the most unconventional of circumstances. The saying, *'You'll find it when you stop looking'* is very appropriate here. Paradise comes to you when you least expect it and it's always hiding behind curtains you never think to draw. Just a note here: the irony of having an outfit ready for something that you're not expecting is not lost on me.

1• 1970s off the-shoulder blue and black floral sheer top
2• 1990s Alannah Hill orange silk gingham skirt
3• Orange and white tasseled Kenzo loafers
4• Adventures in Paradise record by Minnie Riperton

Unexpected paradise

MINNIE RIPERTON ADVENTURES IN PA

Ain't no rhyme for oranges

It's come to a point where I must acknowledge that I was raised pretty much entirely on 1970s television shows, which could potentially have contributed to the aesthetic I favour as an adult. Here, I have to talk about *H.R. Pufnstuf* and the genius of its creators Sid and Marty Krofft.

H.R. Pufnstuf was a late sixties–early seventies television show, with characters consisting of life-size puppets blended in with a 'real boy', Jimmy, and his magical talking flute. Sounds normal. The puppets were mainly animal forms warped somewhat so that humans could stand inside and operate the puppet convincingly. The set was extravagant and designed as a consistent world called Living Island where most inanimate objects had the ability to talk. It's a wild ride, I can tell you.

Anyway, the aesthetic of this television show is so fantastical it is truly something you will never be able to get out of your mind, or out of your nightmares. As well as frightening drama, comforting interpersonal relationships and terrible disguises, the show also offered singing and dancing collaborations between the puppets and the real boy. One of these songs, (all of which were composed originally for the show) was performed by the villainess— Wilhelmina W. Witchiepoo—and it was called '*Ain't No Rhyme For Oranges*'.

This outfit celebrates the brilliant nonsense of *H.R. Pufnstuf* and all the wild imaginings I consequently enjoyed as a child after watching it.

Inspired by Sid & Marty Krofft

1 • 1970s floral-print
baby-doll dress with front
pocket details

2 • Kinki Gerlinki
black-and-white stripe
turtleneck underneath

3 • Kork-Ease leather
platform sandals

TOO
BAD

BAD GIRL

When I went to art school, I became aware of a stereotype which I think began perhaps with Rembrandt or Leonardo da Vinci, and was perpetuated by Jackson Pollock, Pablo Picasso and, nowadays, Jeff Koons and Damien Hirst.

This stereotype is what I like to call the 'Bad Boy Painter'. Bad Boy Painters have little regard for hyglene, because they believe themselves to be otherworldly god-like figures that are above the mere earthly acts of bathing and brushing their teeth. They get about the corridors of art school in tattered, paint-splattered clothes and yet at all times appear to have perfectly-sculpted unsculpted hair. It was not, however, their aesthetic or olfactory issues that I found most problematic, it was how poorly they treated their peers and counterparts (I need not note, particularly women).

After dating a few of these Bad Boy Painters I consider myself somewhat of an expert on the subject. In another life, perhaps I would have dedicated a year to writing a thesis on these not-altogether uncommon anomalies for the benefit of other women in the art world who are bound to encounter them and their antiquated philosophies, overstimulated egos and tendency to ruthlessly break hearts.

This outfit is for Bad *Girl* Painters who could benefit from some ego-stimulation. When I bought this Acne Studios leather jacket (on sale for what was still a small fortune to my bank balance) I immediately felt a surge of self-confidence and power. I put this jacket on when I need reminding that I can do anything, paint anything. I can stand as tall, if not taller, than any old Bad Boy Painter who tries to bring me down.

1• Acne Studios leather
jacket
2• 1970s red knit turtleneck
3• American Apparel black
riding pants
4• Black leather boots
5• Pruda flower
sunglasses

Bad-girl painter

When I think of beatniks I think about words and phrases being monumentally overexaggerated, I think of bongo-drum rhythm and almost-rhymes. Beatniks (as they were labeled by mainstream media) were around from the early fifties to the mid-sixties, a product of Jack Kerouac's writing and musicians such as Bob Dylan.

While I admire their slick style I could never really commit to being one as you have to wear a lot of black and look kind of unimpressed all the time. Nonetheless, it's a fun character to put on every now and then. The leopard-print jacket that I'm wearing here is from Japan in the early 1960s. It's faux fur and the black leopard spots look as though they've been hand-stenciled on. I just love the way it's not perfect: it fits me a little too snugly and the sleeves are awkwardly a little too short.

In my mind, beatniks are kind of blithe and angular, slouching and wearing ill-fitting clothes. My favourite beatnik characters are the ones in John Waters'

1988 film 'Hairspray': they make a brief cameo that leaves one hell of an impression.

This outfit is for an evening at a poetry reading in the cramped, poorly heated basement of a bar in London. Near impossible to find, you wind though dark, wet and slippery cobblestone streets before you eventually come upon a vague yellow light with slim black shadows moving towards it. These are your friends. They're writers, artists and musicians who are basically nocturnal, coming out only after dark if a certain performance is deemed edgy enough to entice them away from their paintbrushes, tambourines and typewriters.

BEATNIK BABY

1 • Thrifted black woollen jumper with diagonal white stripe
2 • 1960s Japanese faux fur leopard print coat
3 • American Apparel black high waisted pants
4 • 1970s rectangular tortoiseshell sunglasses

Sunglasses & tambourines

Beauty School Dropout

There's a line in the 1996 film *Matilda* (based on the novel by Roald Dahl) that is uttered by Matilda's mother to her gentle and nurturing school teacher Miss Honey: 'You chose books, I chose looks.' As if the two are mutually exclusive...

While I believe you can choose both books AND looks at the same time, I still find the notion of the Beauty School Dropout character to be fascinating and I like the fact that they're far more savvy than they give themselves credit for.

Taking inspiration from Matilda's brash, acrylic-nail-wearing mother and of course from the darling Frenchy in *Grease* (1978), this is the ultimate Beauty School Dropout outfit. Floridian in nature, this ensemble is made for golfing while cutting tinting class and perhaps eating fairy floss and strolling along the waterfront.

This outfit is for a chewing-gum-while-walking Beauty School Dropout who lives beyond the label.

Hanging around the corner store

1• 1960s pink halter-neck top with lace detail

2• Milk & Thistle teal gingham print pants

3• Opening Ceremony gingham shoes

Ring my Chimes

Blue Bayou

I went through a phase a few years ago (fewer than you're probably estimating) wherein I was obsessed with the 1970s *Muppet Show*. I was, of course, well above the targeted age bracket; however, I just couldn't tear myself away from those garish sets and those faux-fur-covered puppets.

I bought reissued copies of the show on VHS from a thrift store, and watched it in my spare time (I know, I know). They had such amazing guests, including but certainly not limited to Debbie Harry, Julie Andrews, Harry Belafonte, Petula Clark, Gladys Knight, Diana Ross and, my personal favourite, Linda Ronstadt. The guest on each episode did a number of 'duets' with the muppets. Linda sang 'Blue Bayou' in a set made to look like a swamp, with little frog muppets singing harmony and bopping along in sync with each other. It was pretty much all my most sincere kitsch fantasies together in a three-minute singalong segment.

The song 'Blue Bayou' was originally written and sung by Roy Orbison. It's one of those songs of melancholy and longing that is incredibly familiar and yet you can't quite place it in context. Oddly enough, I find this song optimistic in lots of ways. It washes over you in mists of fondness, daydreaming about a love that used to be and has every opportunity to be again.

This outfit is for being 'all dressed up with nowhere to go', for those nights you end up hugging your knees on your bed and listening to the radio or perhaps longingly leafing through old diaries. It's for fond memories, harking back to something that you wish you didn't screw up and holding onto a glimmer of hope that a piece of that magic can somehow be resurrected.

Tangled up in blue

84

Pastel blue, blue,
navy blue, gold

1• Verner marbled dress
(sample)

2• 1960s gold vintage
sandals

3• 1960s square
gold purse

BOOGIE NIGHTS

It's a bit of a legend in my family that my grandfather, whom I never had the privilege of meeting, went to Studio 54 in 1970s New York and hobnobbed with Barbra Streisand and various other sparkly celebrities underneath the disco ball. I'll go into this story in more detail in the *'Favourite Finds'* section.

In the meantime, this outfit is for a glittering evening at Studio 54 in 1978. Someone beckons you onto the dance floor and 'Got to Be Real' by Cheryl Lynn is playing. You hesitate momentarily before off-loading your glittering purse to a friend and walking, possessed, towards the disco ball.

Got to be real

1 • Gold halter top
2 • Fleur Wood wide-leg
silk pants (remember,
dry clean only)
3 • Massive white cork
platform shoes
4 • 1960s square gold purse

Brandy You're A Fine Girl

'Brandy (You're a Fine Girl)' is a 1972 melancholy pop song by a band called Looking Glass. It has always struck me as particularly sad because it's about a woman who works hard at her job in a bar, and it's near a port or something so lots of sailors come in, and they all tell her how amazing she is and what a good wife she would be but they always leave because apparently they love the sea and their lives as sailors more than they love her.

I like this song because it is catchy but I don't like the way Brandy gets left high and dry by all these dudes who can see how amazing she is but are content with saying goodbye. Brandy is probably feeling really rejected and heartbroken and, like a lot of women, she no doubt gets the raw end of the deal. I think I'd like this song more if it was from Brandy's perspective.

This outfit is about being heartbroken, about loving someone who is far away and has left you in a real state. I'm normally not one to wallow in heartbreak, but unfortunately it is sometimes an unpleasant necessity that shapes you as a person in truly incredible ways. Getting through heartbreak or a breakup makes me feel like I can do ANYTHING, and I don't regret wallowing in a single one.

1• 1970s floral-print tie-up crop top
2• 1970s lurex printed maxiskirt
3• Thrifted cream patent leather Mary Jane shoes

Heartbreak hotel

FOR BRIDGET RILEY...

Bridget Riley is an artist who, in the 1960s, was at the forefront of Op-art.

Op-art is a style of visual art that employs the methods of optical illusion. The works are usually linear, with repeating patterns that appear to the viewer's eyes to be jumpy, moving, or sitting out from the canvas.

Bridget Riley is still a practising artist today, as well as a writer and a curator. She has contributed a lot to the art community, particularly as a woman in the sixties working largely among male artists. Her dynamic, hard-edge paintings demand attention and respect. They switch between making you feel nauseous and unstable and at the same time empowered and steadfast.

This outfit is for camouflaging amid an Op-art survey exhibition in a big stiff white-walled commercial gallery.

Colour Palette

Black and white

1 • 1980s black-and-white striped and spotted cotton maxidress
2 • Swedish Hasbeens black Sky High clogs

Optical illusion

TIME AFTER TIME

I have very vivid memories of New Year's Eve 1999. I was nine years old. My family and I went to my aunt and uncle's house to celebrate the new millennium and my comprehension was that this was a big deal, which I suppose is why so many details stand out to me now. My younger sister had a white bear with 'Y2K' embroidered on it, which she was cradling. We had elaborate masquerade masks that I think my Nanna provided from a party store and I was wearing a knitted pale-blue two-piece top and skirt set with a matching cardigan that I wasn't at all thrilled with.

I stayed up and watched the adults embrace and silently breathe a sigh of relief that the world indeed had not ended and it was okay that we hadn't stockpiled canned food or bottled water. I was excited. My family had a gold-coloured Volvo station wagon for the majority of the time we were growing up. It had a little stained glass hippie sticker on the back windscreen that my mum put there and it also had two extra seats in the boot that faced backwards. It was here that my sisters and I often had to sit, looking out of the back windscreen, when we had extra company.

My most vivid memory of New Year 1999–2000 is going home in the 'very back' of the Volvo with my younger sister, looking out at the drivers in the cars behind us, sometimes waving at them. On this particular trip home, due to the aforementioned excitement, we took to singing the song 'Celebration', by Kool & The Gang, repeatedly. As you can see my taste in music formed very early in life.

This outfit is for ringing in the New Year, perhaps in slightly more adult circumstances than having a singalong in the back of the family car with your sister. I wore this outfit to New Year's Eve 2014 and I recall buying the skirt from Romance Was Born months in advance, knowing that whatever my plans might be for that evening, I was going to be wearing that skirt. It did not disappoint.

Celebration

Auld Lang Syne

1. Georgia Alice off-the-shoulder black silk top
2. Romance Was Born gold tinsel-print silk skirt
3. Black leather boots

Best Western

Peter Pan syndrome

Childlike Empress

In the 1984 film *The NeverEnding Story*, the doe-eyed monarch of Fantasia, the Childlike Empress, seems a symbol of great knowledge and wisdom for one only apparently nine or ten years old. Her character allowed me to think about the body not as an ornate vessel but as a transparent shell, irrelevant and merely serving the purpose of encasing the gold and magic that is inside.

When I was a child I remember imagining myself as an adult, and when I would do so, I would be looking at my adult self as an outsider. I thought that when I 'grew up' I'd lose my way of thinking, that I wouldn't recognise myself. That the certain spark that made me me would disappear with the click of a finger to be replaced by adult thoughts about money and cars or whatever other responsibilities I comprehended adults to have at the time. For a while, to be an adult seemed like a sort of death of the self or a cold, unfriendly reality I'd eventually have to face.

I identified with Michael Jackson's self-professed Peter Pan Syndrome. I identified with Peter Pan himself. I eventually realised, though, that in the real world being eternally youthful is not about not having wrinkles. It's about keeping that spark that dances behind your eyes no matter how many crow's feet border it. It's about a lust for life that oozes out in whatever way you choose to express it. It's about joy, magic and a mild dose of escapism.

This outfit is for intense daydreaming about circumstances far, far away. It's for when your eyes glaze over and you are transported to places that sparkle and shine, guaranteed, each and every time.

1 • 1990s cropped fluffy
silver top
2 • Romance Was Born
pink sequined pants
3 • Funkis white clogs
4 • Thrift store plastic
iridescent beaded
necklace

FactoryGirl

As a teenager, Andy Warhol was my favourite artist. His picture was plastered all over my walls and, thinking about that now, I'm sure my friends and family thought it a little strange that I had images of a silver-haired, sickly looking old man on my wall rather than images of footballers or the members of Good Charlotte. I digress.

It was through my interest in Andy and his work that I inevitably discovered Edie Sedgwick. A disputably dear friend and indisputable muse for Andy, Edie was the ultimate embodiment of sixties cool. I was completely obsessed. I think this obsession sort of aligned with me deciding that I wanted to be an artist: an artist with equal parts Edie and Andy. The idea of the lifestyle, I think, was what initially drew me in. The music and fashion was hypnotically appealing. I either wanted a time machine, or, failing that, to recreate The Factory in my bedroom. I did this very authentically by plastering silver foil over my cupboards; dressing exclusively in vintage swing dresses and big panda eye make-up; sitting on my bed drawing portrait after portrait of Edie Sedgwick.

This long-lasting Andy and Edie fandom gave me the ability to be truly fascinated by people—to see

things as shiny rather than matte—and I'd even go as far as to say that those blurry YouTube videos of Edie partying at The Factory taught me how to dance. Edie Sedgwick's life can be summed up in this Neil Young line: 'It's better to burn out than to fade away'. I think she shone too brightly for this earth. Her shaky voice is haunting and not of this world. After she passed away at the age of 28 she left grains of glitter for us to collect and cherish.

This outfit is for the wildest, most glamorous and most interesting party you've ever been to. The kind you'd wish the parties you went to as a teen were, where people are maintaining intelligent conversations while dancing absentmindedly like heavy ghosts, wearing oddly but fabulously put-together designer concoctions and weighty earrings. Here, the notions of tomorrow or consequences do not exist.

1• 1960s fluffy silver crop top
2• Miu Miu silver, gold and
black leather jacket
3• American Apparel
black disco pants
4• Alpha60 green and
black leather
platform pumps

Life imitates art

FLOWER POWER

My mum is a florist, and a rather good one at that. In the nineties when I was a child, she worked at the biggest and best florist in Melbourne, Kevin O'Neill. She now has her own business. My dad is a very successful garden designer, so between the occupations of both my parents, I was forever (and still am), surrounded by greenery.

Sometimes I would go with mum to visit her workplace; the sensation of walking into the crisply air-conditioned workstations at Kevin O'Neill is still with me to this day. The heady scents of David Austin roses, hyacinths and peonies saturated the air and each breath I took was overwhelmingly euphoric. I would also sometimes go to work with my dad, sitting in the front seat of his car listening to him talk to his employees on the phone and stopping to visit nurseries and sites where his gardens were being constructed. This was more of an earthy experience, with muddy shoes and me wearing my little yellow plastic raincoat and carrying my yellow plastic umbrella, trailing behind dad as he articulated his visions to tradesmen through the dirt.

This outfit is more suited to spending civilised time outdoors, sitting in the shade under a gazebo while sipping lemon, lime and bitters and flipping absentmindedly through the latest *VOGUE Living* magazine.

Peonies, roses & hyacinths

1 • 1970s sheer floral dress with pleated skirt detail
2 • Gorman green suede clogs

Colour Palette

Pink, green, purple, yellow, orange

THINK HAPPY

Stevie Nicks is a warm golden beacon of strength whom I look up to immensely. She's always emanated a particular kind of magic and otherworldly calm that is completely disarming. If you can write a song like 'Landslide', you pretty much have to have superhuman, fine-tuned abilities to read and put words to the most inexplicable and slippery of human emotions. I don't think a single person in the world could deny the profundity of that song.

I liken the presence of Stevie Nicks in this world to a necklace my mum had when I was young. It was called a 'harmony ball' and it is a spherical charm with all these stars and moons over it that makes a soft kind of chiming noise when it moves. I could never for the life of me figure out how it made this noise and quite seriously just put it down to magic.

Stevie Nicks's music, especially her solo stuff, has encouraged me to trust myself and my intuition, to believe in the power of the self, and be unapologetic when it comes to expressing my emotions.

Ths outfit is for a witchy summer's evening underneath a full moon. There's a large bonfire burning in the center of this gathering, and a girl with wild blonde hair is plucking carefully away on her guitar in a corner. You could swear you heard the chiming noise of that necklace your mum had when you were younger, but it could have just been the wind.

Gold and Braid

Her life, her mystery

1• 1970s maxidress with
ruched bodice and
small floral print
2• 1970s brown leather and
rubber wedge platforms
3• 1970s braided bag
4• 1960s Christian Dior
enamel and gold
sunglasses

Good Morning Angels

How I wish I had long flippy seventies hair like Farrah Fawcett. How I wish I could do round kicks and catch bad guys while looking fabulous in a flared jumpsuit and large, rimless seventies sunglasses.

The hair of Charlie's Angels always seem to be blowing in the breeze, even when they were inside. How I wish that were a possibility outside a film set…

I like both the 1970s *Charlie's Angels* television series and the 2000 movie adaptation, which featured the song 'Independent Women' by Destiny's Child on the soundtrack. *Charlie's Angels* to me is less about the actual plotline and more about me watching them, thinking they're awesome and wanting to be them.

This outfit is for 'All the honeys who makin' money'. Thanks, Beyoncé.

1• 1970s light cropped orange jacket
2• Short-sleeve denim overalls
3• Jeffrey Campbell red suede platforms
4• Red heart sunglasses

LOVE

Jumpsuits & high kicks

Colour Palette

Red, orange, denim blue

I used to go to art school

I'm in a band with my friends and fellow artists Jon Campbell and Georgie Glanville. Our band is called Pamela, which just so happens to be my middle name. Georgie and I sing and play the tambourine, and Jon sings and plays the guitar. We play folk–pop songs that are mostly written by Jon, but we have also collaborated on some songs, too. I wrote the lyrics to our hit song, 'Art School' and Jon wrote the melody. It's about my time at the Victorian College of the Arts.

I really enjoy performing with Pamela. My fellow band members are my friends so I am guaranteed to feel confident and at ease when we are up in front of lots of people. Singing is a really enjoyable outlet for me and I love having it as a hobby.

This outfit is for when you're performing in your own offbeat folk–pop band with an inexplicably Australian sensibility. A little nonchalant, a little more often than not out of tune and brash, but always guaranteed to put a smile on your audience's face.

'We'd eat Paddle Pops
Talk on the couch
And we'd drink beer
At the opening of a show
I used to go to art school
Oh yeah I used to go..'

Oh yeah I used to go...

1 • Miu Miu silver, black
and gold leather jacket
2 • 1970s red knit halter top
3 • Romance Was Born
striped pants
4 • Jeffrey Campbell
rainbow
platforms

IT'S GONNA TAKE ALOTTA LOVE

There's a much-quoted line from the effervescent character Penny Lane in the 2000 film *Almost Famous* and it goes like this:

'I always tell the girls, never take it seriously. If ya never take it seriously, ya never get hurt; ya never get hurt, ya always have fun; and if you ever get lonely, just go to the record store and visit your friends.'

'Just go to the record store and visit your friends' is a line that's come up in my mind many a time. It may not be a record store *per se*, just any place where my friends are guaranteed to be, for a back-and-forth chat or a hug and a laugh. The first such instance that I can really recall was when my boyfriend broke up with me at the tender age of sweet 16. My friends were there in an instant, providing me with wisdom and an outlet for my rage, for my nonsensical, irrational rants and, of course, tears. I've made some pretty terrific friends over the years, all of whom I can call on in times of crisis, or any old time, really. All of whom are monumentally important to me and are listed at the back of this book.

You guessed it: this outfit is for going to the record store to visit your dear friends.

Never take it seriously...

Love

1• 1960s green floral cotton minidress
2• Verner marble-print kimono
3• Jeffrey Campbell rainbow platforms
4• Opening Ceremony pink flower sunglasses

I would go so far as to say that Joni Mitchell is my single favourite musician. My mum is a big fan, and literally raised my sisters and me on one cassette tape that had Joni, Carole King and Carly Simon hastily recorded from vinyl records on it.

Once, in primary school, we were instructed to bring in our favourite song for the class. I chose a copy of Joni's 'Big Yellow Taxi' as apposed to the Spice Girls or Eminem, and the teacher played it aloud and told everyone in the class that they 'could learn something from this!'... I was mortified. Now I'm just proud of my younger self for sharing a bit of Joni with kids who wouldn't have otherwise heard it.

Joni, with her angel's voice and her dulcimer (a wooden, four-stringed musical instrument that originated in the Appalachian Mountains of north America) has the most profound affect on me.

Her music demands a pause, a breath: you are then viscerally transported into her world of hurt and celebration and love and warm close dusks at Laurel Canyon in the 1960s. Her music is a dear, dear friend to me and I will never tire of her deep wisdom and richly knitted poetry that can completely destroy you at the same time as building you up again.

This outfit is for a summer afternoon in Laurel Canyon; Joni takes you by the hand to collect wildflowers that you'll place in an antique vase. In Joni's ramshackle house light pours through coloured glass windows and everything is bathed in yellow gold.

Lady of the Canyon

1• Thrifted red gingham cropped top
2• 1970s handmade linen apron dress with pink and green embroidery
3• Gorman green suede clogs
4• 1970s braided basket

Golden afternoon

Looking for a four leaf clover

This outfit is about secrets. It's made for a world where leprechauns exist and pots of gold really do rest at the end of rainbows. I could access this world as a child via mushroom circles in the garden and magic moss-covered corners where I was convinced fairies pranced about every time I turned my back.

A strange sensation washed over me, and my body was drawn inexplicably close: I knelt down where my eyes rested immediately on a perfectly formed and almost-glittering four-leaf clover. I picked it ever so gently and excitedly ran up two stairs at a time to my room, closing the door behind me. The navy blue bookshelf that I shared with my sisters held a menagerie of tales, but it seemed appropriate to reach for the most precious and heaviest book on the highest shelf to house my special find. I slotted the four-leaf clover in the back pages of a copy of *Grimm's Fairy Tales* my aunty had gifted me with, and slid it back into its place.

Only I knew about the lucky clover in there, and I vowed to only go back and find it once it was pressed and dried properly. I think it was months later when I opened the book again in search of my lucky clover, only to find that it was no longer there.

I remember methodically turning through each of the 568 pages of the book in a vain attempt to locate it again. I questioned whether the whole thing had ever even happened: was it just a dream that smoked its way into reality? To this day I don't know if it actually occurred, but it's a memory of mine that I hold quite dear.

Secrets in the garden

Grey, green, dark blue,
blue gingham

1. Green stripy polyester
dress circa 1970s
2. Opening Ceremony
gingham sunglasses
3. Opening Ceremony
blue gingham
shoes

Mushroom Magic

I love the way there's something intrinsically sinister about *Alice's Adventures in Wonderland*. It's a madcap, trippy, unpredictable and ultimately psychedelic tale that was written for children. People seem to make references to it a lot; especially, I found, in high school art class. This happened so much so that I got a bit bored with the whole thing, until I realised that people were making references to it constantly because it was a really major event in their childhood.

As a child, watching the Disney version of *Alice in Wonderland*, reading the book and watching a multitude of other animated and real-life acted versions of the story (including one with Gene Wilder in it) I was engrossed in each rendering. It was such a weird and oddly wonderful display of unfamiliar logic, and it was like something I'd never seen before. Or maybe it was like a bunch of things I'd seen before, but in some weird, lucid dream.

Disney's 1951 animated version has a number of characters that I feel a strange affinity with; all of whom appeared in little poignant vignettes that I could recite word for word to this day. The crying doorknob, the singing flowers, the baby clams who are tragically eaten by the Walrus… my favourite, of course, is the Cheshire Cat. Teasingly menacing with a smile mirroring a crescent moon, the Cheshire Cat incites uneasiness in Alice and in the viewers. The reason for this—I've realised as I've gotten older—is that he's an outsider in Wonderland just like Alice, but he can come and go as he pleases. He's a fascinatingly elusive and very important character perhaps with more involvement in the riddles and nonsense of Wonderland that he would ever let on.

This outfit is for wandering through a hedge maze in a strange, long deserted outer-suburban theme park with the promise of a free game of minigolf if you make it to the end. *If.*

A world of my own

Colour
Palette
Blue, light blue, yellow,
pink, dark blue

1• Romance Was Born
beaded silk
mushroom top
2• Verner marble-print pink
silk dress, worn as a skirt
3• Kinki Gerlinki leather
platform slides with
flower detail

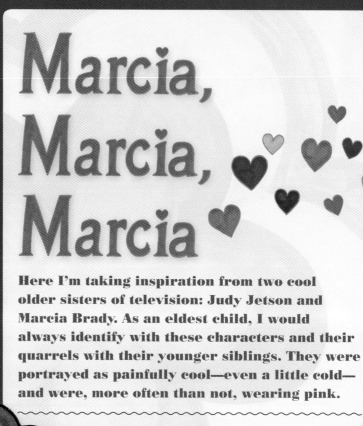

Marcia, Marcia, Marcia

Here I'm taking inspiration from two cool older sisters of television: Judy Jetson and Marcia Brady. As an eldest child, I would always identify with these characters and their quarrels with their younger siblings. They were portrayed as painfully cool—even a little cold— and were, more often than not, wearing pink.

Their dispositions were of certainty and staunch assuredness that I think made viewers have much less compassion for them than their younger counterparts. Older siblings have a way of making it seem like they have it all figured out when, more often than not, they don't. They're just the first to have to do a bunch of those annoying growing-up things and have to learn on their feet.

I want the older sibling to be read as a more sympathetic character, yet still with the same incredible, immaculate style that renders them the 'cool' older sibling. This dress I found in a thrift store long ago—it was maxi length but I took it up to be a mini—and I always found the circular pattern to be very reminiscent of *The Jetsons*. The fuchsia colour was particularly obnoxious and thus perfect.

This outfit is for sashaying through the halls of high school, books clutched close to your chest with what, at the time, feels like the weight of the world on those eldest-sister shoulders.

Eldest sister club

1• 1970s fuchsia
batwing-sleeve dress
2• Funkis white clogs
3• Composition
notebook

This outfit is about chance and taking chances. I've never been much of a risk taker, but as I've gotten older I've tried to encourage myself to venture outside realms that I know to be safe and routine. You can start by taking the smallest of chances and build up your tolerance to not being 100% certain of an outcome. It takes lots of practice to be comfortable with these risks, and it's always important to remember to make relatively calculated ones...

The scariest, most anxiety-inducing chances I've taken is telling a person I like that I like them; but as frightening as it is, I make sure to say it when I feel it. The person on the receiving end should consequently treat me with the same honesty and, whichever way the relationship then goes, I know I said it straight and I won't have any regrets.

This outfit is for telling someone how you feel about them. Your love and affection is the greatest thing you can ever put on a table in front of someone and it takes immense courage to serve it up straight.

Maybe Baby

Take a chance on me

1• Alpha60 blue
midi dress
2• Miu Miu daisy-pattern
shirt underneath
3• Swedish Hasbeens
red leather
T-bars

Mystic Crystal Revelation

This outfit is my homage to the women of the Source Family. The Source Family was a spiritual commune (or, if you're feeling less generous, a cult) that existed in Los Angeles in the 1970s.

The founder and self-appointed leader of this group was a charismatic man known as Father Yod. It all began innocently enough with a health-food store on Sunset Strip. The vast earnings from the popular store allowed Father Yod to rent a mansion in the Hollywood Hills where members of the Source Family all lived communally. As the group gained notoriety and members, Father Yod grew drunk with power. He claimed to be their god; and as their god, he was allowed multiple wives (at one point, he had 14). Members were not allowed access to medicine or doctors, even in childbirth.

In 1974, the Family sold the health-food store and moved to Hawaii. Cracks within the group were beginning to show and it was not the utopian society they once believed in. In 1975, sensing his ultimate demise, Father Yod used a hang glider to leap from a cliff. He crash-landed and, after refusing medical help, died nine hours later. The Source Family slowly disbanded.

This is an abridged version of the story. While I obviously don't agree with the way the members were manipulated, I find it fascinating to delve into the mind spaces of those who were a part of this experience. This cult begun with such good intentions: they strove for a peaceful society where people could exist in harmony with the earth and each other. It's interesting to study where and how this went horribly wrong.

This outfit is for paying a visit to the Source Family's mansion, back in their heyday. You're an outsider allowed a peek into their psychedelic world, but be careful not to get sucked in.

1970s Sunset Strip

1 • 1960s sheer chiffon patterned batwing-sleeve maxidress
2 • Gorman green suede clogs
3 • Thrifted costume jewellery earrings

ORANGE YA GLAD

This outfit is pretty much Dolly Parton's '9 to 5' personified. The song came out in 1980 and, while this is more of a seventies look, it's pretty much exactly the way I imagine the protagonist to be getting around.

The song '9 to 5' is about the office slog, particularly about women making the office slog, and about sexism in the workplace. The lyrics say: 'It's a rich man's game, no matter what they call it, and you spend your life putting money in his wallet.'

This outfit ensures determination and positivity despite you not necessary feeling that way. I'm a big believer in colours dictating your mood, so adorning yourself in orange would account for having a good day at work and maybe even shattering the glass ceiling.

Determination & positivity

1• 1970s orange coat
2• 1990s orange floral print
baby-doll dress with collar
3• Gorman tan clogs
4• Vintage 1970s belt
with gold buckle

Palm Springs

Palm Springs is a desert resort city located in California, USA. I've never visited there, but most of the time I find the most magical places are those you've never been. From what I've read, looked at and imagined, it is the epitome of a pastel-tinted Los Angeles dream world.

Palm trees line the streets, offering a calming stoic presence among the freer spirits of those who reside under their shade: lilting and doe-eyed women wearing muted pinks and greens with slight glints of white. The outfit I've put together is a little flashier than the slightly hippie-esque look I imagine to be prominent in this vignette, but definitely conveys an optimistically peaceful aura, reflected further in the shiny surface of this metallic pink miniskirt I bought from Melbourne label Kinki Gerlinki. The top I bought second-hand at a thrift store, and the palm leaf-like print on the front was obviously very fitting within the context of this outfit.

This outfit is for strolling hand-in-hand with an impermanent lover who may or may not have tousled hair that ever so casually ripples in the slight breeze. I suppose it doesn't matter if the pair of you are actually IN Palm Springs or just somewhere with reasonably manicured green grass and hedges and the towering but friendly authority of a couple of leafy palm trees to affectionately look down on you.

1• 1970s tree-print polyester knit top

2• Kinki Gerlinki shiny pink vinyl skirt

3• Kork-Ease leather platform shoes

4• Thrifted pink-and-white plastic flower bangle

5• Opening Ceremony cat's-eye sunglasses

Peachy Keen

I've always been fascinated by 1950s slang, especially by its delivery in films, usually laced with sarcasm. Rizzo, from the 1978 film *Grease* is my favourite slang user. Her line 'peachy keen, jelly bean' is a standard of mine.

This peach-coloured silk dress is from a Melbourne label called Kinki Gerlinki. I bought it to wear to my exhibition opening in 2012. It's a brilliant dress, as even though it's rather soft and the full skirt falls incredibly delicately, it's actually a very tough-girl dress. Especially paired with this bomber jacket by another Melbourne label, Verner. The combination is super 1950s prom night for the kind of rebel Rizzo character inside us all.

So this outfit is for prom night 1959 with your graduating class. The evening descends and, though summer is looming, the air feels fresh. You hug yourself under the bomber jacket that rests cooly on your shoulders. You and your friends decide to sneak out of the indoor basketball-court-turned-disco for a secret stroll underneath the dome of stars.

Peachy keen, jelly bean

1 • Verner Burning House bomber jacket
2 • Kinki Gerlinki V-back silk prom dress
3 • Swedish Hasbeens red T-bar shoes
4 • Vintage 1990s red headband

I look back fondly on my childhood when I spent much time riding horses, fossicking about outdoors and making up games with my sisters. I always identify with characters who've had simple, uncomplicated upbringings with lots of time for for imagination and entertaining themselves.

I think a lot of creative people have come from such backgrounds. On my horse I spent a lot of quite time observing, thinking, distance-staring and daydreaming. In retrospect, these absent-minded moments were very formative.

When I was a child I distinctly remember watching the 1937 Shirley Temple film, *Heidi*, in black and white on VHS at my Nanna's house. When I was a little older I read the book, and really felt some kind of affinity with Heidi. She's so industrious and bright and thrives in her sparse environment.

I believe that some people are just born with a spark, and no matter what circumstances they find themselves in, they continuously do right by others, and spread joy and optimism. That's kind of my definition of a Prairie Girl, anyway. It's about keeping things simple and placing renewed importance on basic core values.

This outfit is for times when you're outdoors and you're looking at something far in the distance, but the sun is so bright that you need to shade your eyes with your hand to stop yourself squinting.

Prairie Girl

Gingham & daisy chains

1. 1970s red cotton daisy-print dress with black velvet bow
2. Swedish Husbeens red 1-bar clogs
3. Red silk head scarf

The Girl

135

RENAISSANCE WOMAN

Time is a fascinating thing. I have long been obsessed with the way it has the ability to alter perceptions of memories, but mostly the way that if enough of it goes by, it tends to continue to come around in a circle. I am enamoured by the 1960s and 1970s (if you can't already tell) and what is particularly interesting to me is that the seventies bands that I enjoy, such as Led Zeppelin, Jethro Tull and Pentangle, were incorporating medieval, renaissance and baroque elements into their music. It was called 'medieval folk rock'.

The action of harking back to past inspiration and cutting pieces of that and pasting them into a contemporary context is what I like to do with lots of things in my life, such as fashion and art. If I happen to be inspired by a particular Led Zeppelin song and use inspiration from that to make an artwork, then I'm technically also inspired by the renaissance, and everything becomes a big giant cut-and-paste-fest of returning and borrowing. In time, the work I've made may be of inspiration to someone else, and the cycle goes on forever.

This outfit is for being backstage at some big folk rock festival, perhaps the infamous Woodstock. Your long-haired boyfriend of rock-star fame is about to go out on stage to face the screaming and muddy masses, so you throw him your jacket to wear for good luck.

Woodstock & folk rock

Colour Palette

Gold, orange, yellows burnt sienna, brown, browny red

1 • Miu Miu silver, gold and black leather jacket
2 • 1970s maxidress with renaissance woman print
3 • 1960s gold sandals

'She would never say where she came from. Yesterday don't matter if it's gone.'

I cite 'Ruby Tuesday' as the second-most heartbreaking Rolling Stones song. Written by Keith Richards in a Los Angeles hotel room, it is allegedly about a woman who flew in and out of his sphere all too quickly.

This outfit is for navigating long and lonely highways with gritty feet and sun soaked shoulders. Unsure of your destination, you stop at the curb of a long deserted roadside diner to re-evaluate your route and try to hitch your next ride. Resting gratefully on your suitcase, you squint beneath your sunglasses to make out a pale blue Country Sedan snaking your way. As it comes closer you stick out your thumb, uncaring of destination or duration of this potential ride. As long as you are covering ground you can continue to believe you can fly. Suitcase first, sliding in, you take off along the highway, wind down your window and stick your arm out and let the wind catch it like it's a wing.

Goodbye Ruby Tuesday

Love is the Drug

Pink, metallic pink, red, metallic red

1• 1970s knitted red halter top
2• 1960s pink lurex skirt
3• Swedish Hasbeens red T-Bar clogs
4• Thrifted 1960s stickered suitcase

TIME AFTER TIME

139

SIREN SONG

There's a magical place in Florida that I've only read about. It's a famous waterpark that was founded in 1947 and features 'mermaids' (well, women dressed in fish tails and wearing elaborate, sparkling costumes). They perform daily in the Weeki Wachee Springs in front of audiences who view the show through a large glass window not unlike an aquarium.

YouTube videos show that their athleticism is pretty outstanding, but what I really enjoy is that fact that these women are pretty much the closest thing to real-life embodiment of actual mermaids.

I have always harboured a bit of a fascination with mermaids, ever since I was a child and watched a VHS copy of Disney's *The Little Mermaid*, I felt a real affinity with Ariel, an affinity based pretty much solely upon the fact that she had red hair like me. The mermaids in Disney's *Peter Pan* almost scared me, on the other hand, and I think the thing about mermaids as a legend and concept is that they are mesmerisingly enigmatic and draw you in, only to subtly destroy you. And THAT'S exactly what I like about them. They are female characters who have been around for hundreds of years, whose good looks do not equate with them being dippy or incapable. They're fierce and although they live in water they have fire burning hot behind their eyes.

This outfit is for less sinister notions of perhaps taking a trip to Weeki Wachee Springs, or spending a day lounging on a plastic pink 1960s banana lounge with a drink that has one of those mini umbrellas in it.

Weeki Wachee Springs

1• 1960s polyester pink knit
knit T-shirt
2• Tsumori Chisato
mermaid-print maxiskirt
3• Gorman green
suede clogs
4• Opening Ceremony
pink flower glasses
5• 1960s shell purse

Soul Train is probably one of the most spectacular television shows I've ever seen. Other people agreed, and it ran for a massive 35 years from 1971 to 2006. *Soul Train* is an American musical variety show, featuring performers primarily singing R&B, soul, funk, jazz, disco and hip-hop.

In the seventies, not only were the performers on the show brilliant—singers like Freda Payne, Stevie Wonder and The Jackson 5—but the format of the show had dancers positioned around the stage, dancing freely and largely unchoreographed to the music. There's nothing more liberating to watch than these athletic and exceptionally talented dancers.

On a dance floor I wish I had even a quarter of the ability that they have. Not only is there the dancing to watch, and the performer of course (whom I've long ago forgotten about in favour of the dancers)

it is also a really concise snapshot of the grooviest fashions of the time. Watching old clips of *Soul Train* is a much more satisfying way to watch musicians perform. The dancers make the environment feel accessible and ultimately human and it looks like so much fun that I can barely contain myself.

This outfit is for watching *Soul Train* on your television in the 1970s—kind of like Tracey Turnblad watching 'The Corny Collins Show' in John Waters' *Hairspray*—wishing, hoping and praying to be involved somehow in this magic wonderland beyond the screen.

SOUL Train

Groovin' on a Sunday afternoon

1 • 1970s red polyester knit top with black and white trim
2 • 1970s denim patch-print skirt
3 • 1960s gold sandals
4 • Badges designed by me

SOUL

Suffragette City

This outfit is an indirect homage to my favourite 'Sister Suffragette'. Her name is Winifred Banks, but you will probably know her as the mother of Jane and Michael in the 1964 *Mary Poppins* film.

She's a complete rocket in a petticoat and I think if she existed when David Bowie was around singing 'Suffragette City' she may have dressed a little more on the wild side in something not dissimilar to this.

This outfit is for when you're walking down the same boring old street you always walk down but you want it to feel like a runway.

'Our daughters' daughters will adore us, and they'll sing in grateful chorus: "Well done, sister suffragettes"!'

Soldiers in petticoats

1• Gorman pink and black patterned jumpsuit (sample)
2• Black leather boots

SUSPICIOUS MINDS

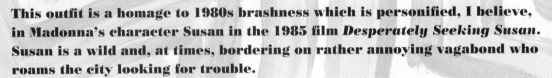

This outfit is a homage to 1980s brashness which is personified, I believe, in Madonna's character Susan in the 1985 film *Desperately Seeking Susan*. Susan is a wild and, at times, bordering on rather annoying vagabond who roams the city looking for trouble.

There is a scene that I have a particular fondness for, when Susan has just been washing herself in a public toilet and turns the hand dryer upward to casually dry her underarms while chewing gum. She's so irreverent and obnoxious and it's completely charming.

What I like about Madonna when she acts (and what most people don't like about Madonna when she acts) is that there is so much of her as a person still there. She combines her characters with herself

so they always have that unapologetic brashness present that has been cited as making her world-famous and at the same time very controversial.

This outfit is for standing on street corners in New York City with nothing much to do; for hanging around, chewing gum and eating snacks with a very slight smirk on your face. You've no money but have faith that your presence on the street corner is enough of a catalyst for something of interest to occur.

SUSPICIOUS
MINDS

1• Opening Ceremony pink
Suspicious Minds jumper
2• 1980s acid-wash
denim skirt
3• Mercibeautcoup
pink platform shoes
4• Opening Ceremony
gingham sunglasses

Looking for trouble

THe PiaNO LessoN

When I was a child my Aunty Em (yes, just like in *The Wizard of Oz*) used to give me informal lessons.

These lessons would vary from being taught Russian (she is fluent in the language) to studying paintings in big heavy art books that she would lay out on her four-poster bed. I was never really enamoured with the Russian language.

The paintings, of course, I was fascinated by. I can remember vividly all those that we discussed. From Arthur Boyd's Brides to *Portrait of an Unknown Woman* by Ivan Kramskoi to the work of Paul Klee. When Aunty Em was living in Russia, she would send me postcards of paintings that I would be instructed to write about. One postcard that she sent was of Matisse's *The Piano Lesson*, which to date I would say is one of my favourite paintings. It depicts a young boy seated at a piano with a kindly figure of a woman, presumably the piano teacher, in the background. The colours are delightfully muted: greys, greens, blues and an orangey–pink with black line detail. It's stunning. I cite my first look at a mere reproduction of this painting as the first time I thought about art in a very serious way. I was young, but I was so baffled by the number of thoughts I could have from this one image, that I was completely hooked.

This outfit is for a tranquil and rich encounter with an artwork. They are rare these days, but I recommend going back to heavy art books spread out on your bed rather than a busy and glittery exhibition opening or a Google image search.

1• 'Dress up' black
silk top
2• Acne Studios wide-leg
printed cotton pants
3• Swedish Hasbeens
black clogs

Inspired by Matisse

'Tiptoe Through the Tulips' is a song originally written and recorded in 1929. It was more prominently covered by musician Tiny Tim in 1968. I have a real fondness for Tiny Tim: looking past his could-be-construed-as-irritating falsetto voice, I think he was a fascinating performance artist.

He had an *Alice in Wonderland*-like presence, sinister and haunting vibes masked underneath a haphazardly comedic exterior. The print on this 1970s cotton tie-up top immediately lent itself to being a tribute to Tiny Tim and his rendition of '*Tiptoe Through the Tulips*', so when I came across it at a thrift store one Sunday afternoon I couldn't resist. The slightly bell-shaped sleeves would be very appropriate for shaking maracas *a la* Peter Allen in 'I Go To Rio', and it's just generally a little funny but a lot of fun.

This outfit is for tiptoeing joyously among fields of blooms, perhaps not as gracefully as one would like. It's twee and daggy, but, if you OWN it—like perhaps openly harbouring some kind of obsessive Tiny Tim fandom—it's also completely fabulous.

TIPTOE THROUGH THE TULIPS

1. Tulip patterned cotton tie-up top, circa 1970s
2. Gorman wide-leg black raw silk cocktail pants
3. Swedish Hasbeens red shoes

Curiouser & curiouser

upside down umbrellas

Okay, sometimes I think it is really boring when people recite their dreams to me. While I'm fascinated by my *own* dreams, when someone else starts rattling off one of theirs I find myself tapping my finger on my non-existent wrist watch. As self-absorbed as this makes me seem, I stand by my statement.

When people make art out of their dreams, however, it is a different story. That I find captivating. Films like Robert Altman's 1977 *3 Women*, with Sissy Spacek and Shelley Duvall (my favourite actors) and some of the scariest scenes in David Lynch's 1990s television series *Twin Peaks* are cinematic examples of art inspired by and/or about dreams. In art, surrealism is the movement closely aligned with dreams. Figures like Salvador Dali, Dorothea Tanning and Leonora Carrington painted lucidly on canvas scenes of melting chaos.

René Magritte, a Belgian surrealist, has probably produced my favourite examples of surrealism. When the clothing label Opening Ceremony announced a line of clothing featuring prints of his work, I was so excited. My sister brought back this top for me when she went on a trip to New York, and it's as much a piece of art as it is an item of clothing.

This outfit is for embracing the silliness of surrealism and largely ignoring the sinister, scarier elements. Surrealism is witty and thought-provoking and doesn't have to be entirely about disappearing down the rabbit hole of one's wildest dreams. If it challenges the viewer's ideas of 'normal' and their perceptions of reality, it has served its purpose.

Dreamy surrealism

154

Love is the Drug

1 • Opening Ceremony Magritte umbrella-print top
2 • Tsumori Chisato printed silk pants
3 • Swedish Hasbeens Slip In Classic clogs

Venus in Blue Jeans

This pair of jeans I have had for many, many years. They're vintage Levi's that I found at a thrift store. They're the kind of pants that feel like they were individually tailored for me.

I wear them when I have an exhibition to install, hence the paint stains; they're perfect, and after accompanying me to many a messy exhibition installation and studio move, I can also say that they're a good-luck charm to boot.

This outfit is an ode to the old favourites, an ode to feeling fabulous and powerful in your oldest, dirtiest and worn-out clothes that have never let you down and never will.

Mona Lisa with a ponytail

1• Antipodium bear-print
bomber jacket
2• 1970s blue lurex
sleeveless top
3• 1980s vintage
Levi's jeans
4• Black leather boots

Ring my Chimes

VOULEZ-VOUS

I am a big ABBA fan. A part of me feels that this announcement should have been prefaced with, 'I have a confession to make', but you know what? Contrary to the way I've been made to feel my whole life, ABBA is a band you need not be ashamed to like.

Yes. They're 'daggy', but daggy in my mind is near brilliant: daggy is what everyone is thinking but not game enough to say, it is familiar and of another world at the same time...

Songs by ABBA completely transcend time and space. They are—I'm not going to say timeless—forever relevant, or something. Their sentiments are solid. The songs evoke a sort of sonic primary-colour simplicity that not many people can dismiss.

This outfit is for a *Muriel's Wedding*-type moment of clarity: and here I quote Muriel herself: 'since I've met you and moved to Sydney, I haven't listened to one ABBA song. That's because my life is as good as an ABBA song. It's as good as "Dancing Queen".'

Take it now or leave it

ABBA GIFT BOOK
Everything about YOUR favourite group INSIDE!

1 • Alpha60
pale blue linen
off-shoulder top
2 • Dress Up red
Liner skirt
3 • Peter Jensen
platform wedges

I love watching *The Brady Bunch*. I have since I was a child. It was as much of a familiar television show that I grew up with as if I'd grown up in the seventies. It's pretty scary, but I know most episodes by heart. Anyway, once I realised that, I became aware that I had a problem on my hands. They're not making any new *Brady Bunch* episodes anymore and, unsatisfied with knowing all the words and outcomes of the gripping plot lines, I had nowhere else to get my fix. That is, until I discovered *The Brady Bunch Variety Hour*.

The Brady Bunch Variety Hour is a television show that is exactly what its title prepares you for. An hour-long musical variety show that features all of the original cast of *The Brady Bunch* (except Eve Plumb, the actress who played Jan Brady. Turns out she knew when to leave on a high note) after the original television show's fifth and last season.

It is truly the most breathtakingly tacky and simultaneously brilliant thing I've ever watched. I say this with the utmost sincerity. It is amazingly obnoxious, oh-so-terribly scripted and features THE most daggy 1970s choreography to have ever existed. Because of all this, it's only the best thing I've ever laid eyes on. It's all-singing, all-dancing, all-off-key and out-of-time (thanks to *The Brady Bunch* who have had no formal musical training) and it's MY FAVOURITE THING EVER.

My descriptions don't do it justice; it truly has to be experienced. There are clips on YouTube you can appropriately pore over in your spare time. There are only nine episodes because the production costs were so astronomical for something that really wasn't super-popular in its time. In 2002, it was voted number four in a *TV Guide* compilation of the 50 worst TV shows of all time.

I digress. What I really enjoy about these kinds of elaborate seventies stage productions is the enthusiasm that the cast and crew had for making something so enormously and unapologetically BIG. Their philosophy is so clearly 'more is more' and I, for one, really respect that.

This outfit is for a debauched evening of singing karaoke to unapologetically BIG retro songs such as 'Xanadu' by Olivia Newton-John or anything by the Bee Gees. The cramped room is filled with disco lights that flicker softly over your face in perfect sync with the music. Black-and-white zebra-print wallpaper complements perfectly with the fuchsia shag carpet. If you look closely, there are lots of stains on the rug and the wallpaper is rather filthy, but this is not the night for studying things intently. It's about glitter and trick mirrors and having the best fun of your life despite how terrible the tune that you carry may be.

XANADU

Red, maroon, white, rainbow

1• Kenzo red lurex jumpsuit
2• Jeffrey Campbell rainbow platforms
3• Thrifted heart-shaped sunglasses

A place where nobody dared to go

Favourite
Finds

Favourite Finds

It's strange, but sometimes I feel an odd, inexplicable pull towards particular objects. For example, if I am innocently browsing through racks at an op shop (thrift store), I could have a feeling as though I should look behind something, or check out something I can see peeking out of a corner. Usually, if I have that baffling but undeniable urge it results in me finding something really special. I know it sounds crazy, but sometimes I definitely believe in some sort of op shopping intuition.

Okay, so op shopping intuition might just be a product of my overactive imagination, but there have been multiple instances where it's been apparent. I have a tendency to delve into theories of psychometry— a form of extrasensory perception otherwise known as token-object reading—whereby one picks up an object and is able to know past circumstances and situations it has been in. While the theory is reliant on being pretty open-minded, sometimes I do like to think that's the reason why I stumble across particular objects that just seem meant for me.

What I like about op shopping is that every object or garment you come across has a level of emotional weight to it. It is a porous surface for human experience and everything you touch has traces of others who have touched it before. (Don't think of this in terms of germs: you'll go a bit mad on hand sanitiser if you do.) Anyway, I think this spirit of sharing and this idea of making an experience collective via a passing-down of objects is at the core of my love for op shopping and collecting.

I simply couldn't resist having a section in this book that highlights some of my absolute favourite finds. Most of them are not valuable, and are kitschy and funny, but they are the sorts of things I treasure and cherish for years. They contribute to a lightness of being, a sense of fun, and they are the things that clutter and inhabit all the surfaces in my bedroom…

Favourite Finds

ABBA wall-hanging

I think my obsession with ABBA has previously been touched upon in this book, but here we go again... I bought this ABBA-printed fabric wall-hanging from a vintage store that used to be near my work. I'd go there on my lunch break for a browse and I found it very therapeutic. One day I found this, and knew it had to hang on one of my already chock-a-block walls. Agnetha is my favourite member of ABBA. If I could trade my entire wardrobe for hers in the sixties and seventies, oh, I would. In the picture on the wall-hanging she's not wearing anything particularly remarkable, but there's this incredible outfit of hers that is pretty much burned into my memory. It's a vibrant pink skin-tight jumpsuit with a heart cut out of the stomach with rhinestones around it. It's just the greatest thing I've ever seen and if, in many years' time, that jumpsuit comes up at some kind of auction and I am in a financial position to buy it, I will.

Anyway, this wall-hanging is threadbare and practically see-through so it's very fragile. I have to be careful with it, but it's a great example of the extent of ABBA fandom in the 1970s and I really love it.

Barbie cases

I've found two 1960s Barbie cases in my thrifting travels. One was at a market, and I bought it to put my felt-tip colouring pens in. The other was at Savers, and when I first picked it up it felt unusually heavy. When I opened it, there lay someone's Barbie and entire Barbie wardrobe, untouched for about 50 years.

Okay, so Barbie's arm was broken and her hair was half detached, but in my eyes it was a brilliant sight to behold. How had this Barbie case just been packed up, mid-imaginative game, and never opened again? I imagined a girl on the cusp of her teen years beginning to feel detached from her once-cherished doll. Perhaps she got it out one last time, to dress the doll she'd once named and spent countless hours with before eventually laying her to rest. Dust collected and the case was shoved further and further back into the wardrobe until many years later, when she was shunted off to Savers for me to stumble across.

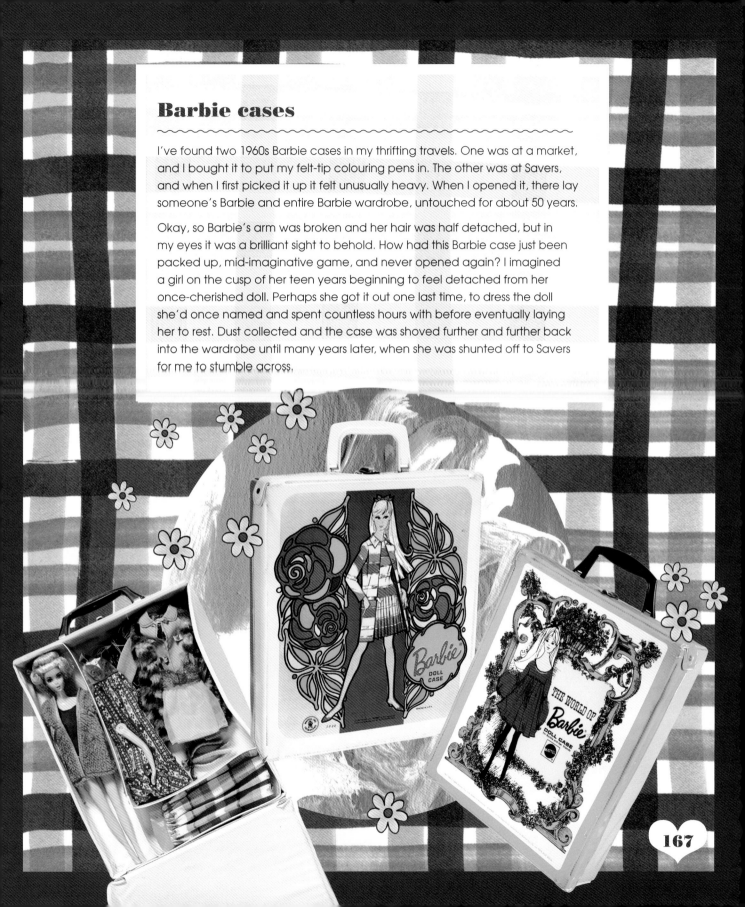

Favourite Finds

Barbra Streisand record

My grandfather spent some time in New York in the 1970s, and this was the gift he bought back for his daughter (my aunt). It's a signed Barbra Streisand record. After meeting her producer at the infamous Studio 54 nightclub, he was invited the next day to a recording session with Barbra, where he met her and asked her to sign the record. I love this story, because I can just imagine how precious and treasured this object would have been (and, well, still is) and how impressive it must have seemed. Coming back to Australia from the 'Big Apple', having met Barbra Streisand, would have been the greatest party story and I only wish it were my own to tell.

168

Cream record album

I found this record at Savers (surprise, surprise). It was in the little locked glass cabinet they have which is reserved for objects they deem to be 'antique' or 'valuable', but truly this album is one of the only good things I've ever picked out of there. Anyway, I'd wanted this album for ages, not because I'm a particularly big Cream fan but because I'm a HUGE fan of Martin Sharp, who was an Australian artist, and he just so happened to have designed this album cover. He was active from the 1960s right up until his death in late 2013 and he's my idol because he worked across the fields of commercial illustration and fine art. His works are psychedelic and kaleidoscopic and, often at the same time, they are political and controversial.

In August of 2013, I had the privilege of being in an exhibition with Martin Sharp. Titled 'Graceland', it was a group show dedicated to Elvis Presley, held at Damien Minton Gallery in Sydney. Martin exhibited one piece: a large-scale painting of Elvis Presley that he'd been working on for a number of years. His declining health meant it was incredibly hard for him to physically make work, and this painting was no mean feat. I exhibited a fabric print of a collage I'd made of Elvis Presley, and the two works—Martin Sharp's and mine—hung side by side. I was beyond stoked to be included in an exhibition with Martin. Unfortunately, I wasn't able to travel up to Sydney at the time of the exhibition opening and was unable to meet him. In December of the same year, Martin Sharp passed away, and I will always regret not meeting him when I had the opportunity. I take comfort, though, in the fact that our works had some sort of relationship while they were hanging together in the gallery.

Favourite Finds

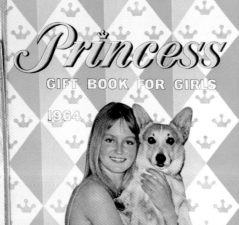

Girl's Annual books

This is not a super-specific 'Favourite Find': it's more a type of book for which I'm always on the lookout when I'm rifling through second-hand book shops. They're called *Annuals* and were made as gift books for girls, with comics, stories, craft activities, general knowledge, crosswords, etcetera. Some of my favourite types of these books are those published in the 1960s and 1970s, because they have the most dynamic illustrations with brilliant, fearless colours.

I've grown a pretty vast collection of these books over the years and my favourites include those pictured. They're great to pore through on rainy days through the lens of a twenty-first century person, because it's important to be very conscious and critical of the abhorrent sexism and the lack of representation of women of colour throughout the pages.

Favourite Finds

I HAD A BAG
OF FUN
IN

at
Halls Gap

I had a bag of fun in...

I come across some pretty great things while I'm op shopping. I have also come across some pretty odd things. This little ceramic pencil holder made me laugh out loud when I saw it, basically because it's so grammatically incorrect and bizarre. I don't think I've ever been to Halls Gap, but I doubt an owl sitting on a paper bag has anything to do with the Victorian country town. Also, the owner of some dodgy tourist shop has obviously bought a bunch of these owls sitting on paper bags and carefully handpainted 'at Halls Gap' on the front to customise it for their clientele. The whole thing reads 'I had a bag of fun in at Halls Gap' and it's so hilariously bad that I love it. Looking at it is always guaranteed to make me laugh.

Joni Mitchell *Song to a Seagull* record

This record is the BEST record I've ever found at Savers. My love for Joni Mitchell is touched upon in this book, which explains why I was so fervent when I pulled this gem out of the stacks of the many dusty Nana Mouskouri records. This is actually, like, a kind of rare Joni Mitchell record: it's her first album, pressed in 1968. The cover illustration is done by Joni herself, and it is so intricate and calmingly beautiful to stare at. The back cover I like even more, it has more of the vine-like line work circling a fish-eye photograph of Joni holding a red umbrella in a rainy street.

This is a very, very special object of mine not only because of its beauty but because I found it so very long ago, in a very formative teenage period of my life. I think I was 16, and at the time it was such a warm, important little light at the end of a tunnel that I found in my suburban Savers store.

Favourite Finds

Key-shaped ring

This is a 1970s Avon-brand sterling silver ring. In the sixties and seventies, Avon products were sold door to door, and they manufactured things like perfumes, jewellery, ceramics and even glassware, as well as the make-up that they continue to produce today. This ring was my mum's: when she was 15 she was one of the door-to-door Avon salespeople. She seems to recall that the ring was a gift for selling a certain amount of product. I'd like to say that she gave me this ring, but I'm pretty sure I just commandeered it when I found it one day while rifling through her things. I wore it religiously from when I was 16 to 18 and I thought it was the coolest thing since sliced bread.

I mean, it is, right? It's a ring shaped like a key. I used to imagine that it was the (get this) 'key to my heart' and when I met someone whom I fell in love with I'd stop wearing the ring. When I think of that now it's, like, super-sweet but man, I was so super-corny and had evidently watched way too many Disney movies! Pretty sure I got sick of wearing the key to my heart on my finger every day before I actually fell in love, so I ditched it and it's been sitting in my bedside table drawer ever since.

Leonardo DiCaprio necklace

I found this necklace in a really tiny thrift store in a really tiny town. I was just about to leave empty-handed when I took a glance at the jewellery cabinet and this caught my eye. I think I paid 20 cents for it, which is a minuscule price for something that so brilliantly encapsulates the 1990s. I love anything that really captures intense fandom, particularly around the time of the Spice Girls and Hanson. Obsession is the correct word for it, really. The person who owned this necklace probably had a plethora of Leonardo DiCaprio merchandise, wore this necklace every day and kissed a life-size poster of him every night before she fell asleep. I hope that was the case, anyway.

Favourite Finds

The BIOGRAPHY
ROBERT MATTHEW WALKER

Madonna memorabilia

Not many people know that I am a huge Madonna fan. I have been since I was 14 years old. I always knew of her music, but I remember watching her performing in a white pants suit at *Live 8* in 2005, and I was completely and utterly captivated. I still can't pinpoint what it was, specifically, about that performance that thrust me into the role of full-blown Madonna fangirl. Since then I've read every Madonna biography, collected badges, tapes, records, videos, books, stickers, iron-on patches… If it had something to do with Madonna, I had to have it. I'm a little embarrassed about this part, but when I was 14 I had a Madonna fan website where I would just, like, upload pictures of Madonna that I'd saved off the internet… It was crazy. Anyway, I still love Madonna, but it's not teenage-fan level anymore. She has said and done some problematic things over the past few years, but I continue to admire her as a woman who's over the generally 'accepted' age a woman should be in pop music, and refuses to listen to those telling her to shut up and fade into a comfortable and modest life. Just because a woman gets to a particular age, it does not mean she should disappear. And I will always support Madonna in her releasing pop music and performing and dancing in whatever clothes she wants to until whatever age she pleases.

Anyway, here is just some of my treasured and vast collection…

Man & Woman encyclopedia

This book was a really remarkable find. It's a book published in 1970 and it is about sex. While reading through I expected a rather conservative account but was pleasantly surprised. It's a very progressive publication for having been released in the seventies. It accounts for a woman's perspective on sex, which is something that I believe at that time was largely ignored, or, at least only beginning to be explored.

Not only is this book quite radical for its time but it's also filled with beautiful photographs and illustrations. This is one of those special books that (yes, don't worry) I'll never cut up for collage.

Favourite Finds

1960s inflatable plastic coathangers

My friend Brodie found a packet of these 1960s inflatable coathangers for me at a New York flea market. When she brought them back as a present I was visibly thrilled that someone knew my aesthetic and interests in obscure retro knick-knacks so well. I was so excited, in fact, that I didn't wash the mouthpiece before inflating them… Should I be concerned that I've picked up some 1960s avian flu that was lying dormant on this one packet of inflatable coathangers? Hmm, probably. It was worth it because they're just so pretty, not to mention practical!

1960s Christian Dior sunglasses

When I came across these sunglasses online, I had to have them. I HAD to have them. These urges are dangerous because if I have to have something but I don't happen to have a lot of money, I delve right into my savings to make any purchase possible. This was one of those times. And it was worth it.

When I received them in the mail I'd never been so excited to open any parcel before. These are more than just sunglasses: they're sort of an art object, so intricately crafted with gold and enamel. I can imagine the beautiful woman who looked through these lenses in the sixties, out onto a rolling rose-tinted landscape.

These sunglasses are special to me not because of their market value but because of their rarity and craftsmanship. They have so much weight to them, and they've been so cherished. I will continue to do so.

179

Favourite Finds

Memory Motel necklace

I decided at some point after I left university and started exhibiting my work, that I'd get a custom necklace made with the title of every solo exhibition I did. These are two of them. One reads 'Memory Motel', which was an exhibition I had at the beginning of 2014; the other reads 'Feel Flows' which was the title of an exhibition I had early 2013. It's a really daggy little tradition that I began, and it's just cheap costume jewelry, but they are such sweet and sentimental little mementoes and I keep them hanging on my wall to spark fond memories of the different bodies of work I've let out into the world.

Miniature Barbie record player

This teeny-tiny record player from the 1960s was my mum's when she was growing up. It's a Barbie record player, complete with a little removable cardboard record and plastic stylus that you can lift on and off. My Mum tells me of a fascination with small, doll-sized objects that she harboured. This little record player was one of her favourites, which is probably why it has stuck around for all these years.

I think it wound its way into the Barbie box I shared with my sister when we were growing up, and I was always interested in trying to read the writing on the record. It's completely minuscule but to this day I'm convinced it says something significant.

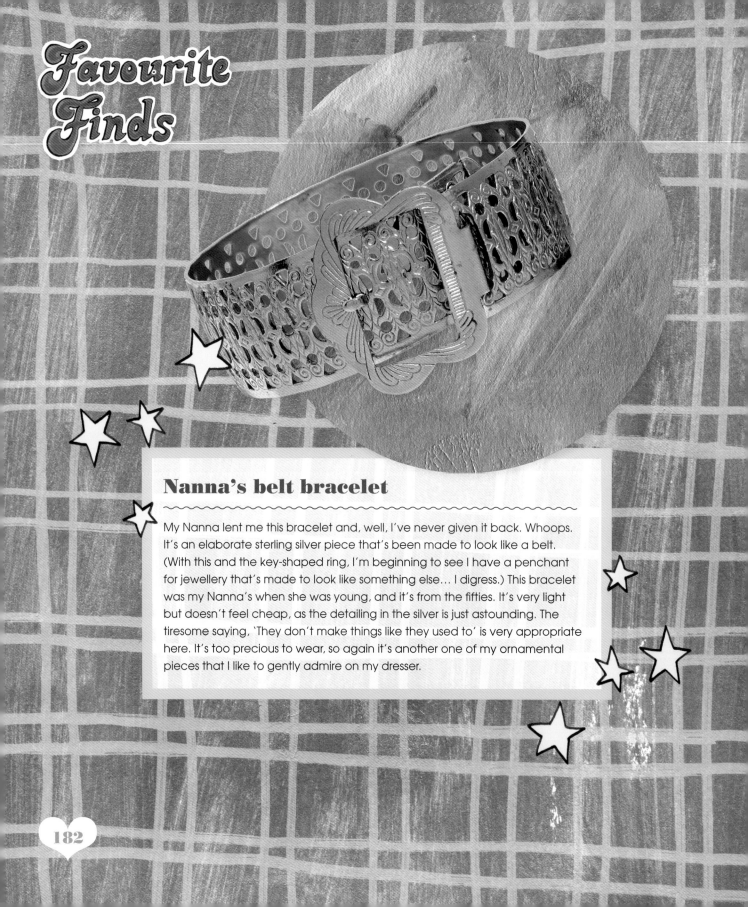

Favourite Finds

Nanna's belt bracelet

My Nanna lent me this bracelet and, well, I've never given it back. Whoops.
It's an elaborate sterling silver piece that's been made to look like a belt.
(With this and the key-shaped ring, I'm beginning to see I have a penchant
for jewellery that's made to look like something else… I digress.) This bracelet
was my Nanna's when she was young, and it's from the fifties. It's very light
but doesn't feel cheap, as the detailing in the silver is just astounding. The
tiresome saying, 'They don't make things like they used to' is very appropriate
here. It's too precious to wear, so again it's another one of my ornamental
pieces that I like to gently admire on my dresser.

Plastic 'Chip' McDonald's toy

This is probably the item that I've had for the longest out of everything in this book. It's a McDonald's Happy Meal toy from when I was a kid and *Beauty and the Beast* came out at the movies. It's a character called Chip from the film. I would have been one year old when the movie was released, but I remember receiving a copy of it on VHS from my uncle the following Christmas. I reckon it was the only video I had at the time and I would watch it over and over and over and over again. Another early memory I have relating to *Beauty and the Beast* is that my Dad was designing the garden of this guy who conducted the orchestra at a big *Beauty and the Beast* stage show, so he was given some tickets and he took me. I was infatuated because it was the first thing I'd seen live on stage. I don't know if this part is something I've gradually made up, but I think the conductor looked out of the pit and waved at us! I may have to check this with my dad… Anyway, after the show was over we went back to our car to find it was being towed away because we'd parked in a tow-away zone, and we got a ride back home in the tow truck. Me sitting up there like Jackie O in the middle seat dreaming about *Beauty and the Beast*.

Oddly enough after remembering all these little snippets, I don't actually remember GETTING this Happy Meal toy; but these *Beauty and the Beast*-entwined fond memories explain why such a cute but crappy little plastic thing has stuck around for all these years.

Favourite Finds

Plastic sheep and lamb toys

These 1960s plastic squeaky toys are more creepy than they are cool, I think, but I couldn't resist when I found them at a market. The head of the blue one turns around 360 degrees and I'm pretty sure one night I'll wake up, sitting bolt upright as its eyes will be glowing red and its head will turn around and look at me or something…

Red 1970s plastic pendant

This necklace was given to me in 2011 at the end of my third year at university by Janenne Eaton, an artist and the head of the painting department at the Victorian College of the Arts. I admire her immensely as a beacon of pure uncompromising strength and determination. It was well known that she did NOT take any crap around the studios, and while on one hand the students were mildly terrified of her they equally felt as open and respectful towards her as most of us do our own mothers. She is a force to be reckoned with and someone I cite as an inspirational figure in my early years of 'being an artist'.

Janenne said she had this necklace in the 1970s and it was special to her. After all, she'd kept it since then. I was pretty stoked that she chose to pass it on to me. It has become a bit of a good luck charm and I wore it to my interview to get into Honours. It hangs ornamentally on my wall in my studio, and I daydream about all the brilliant places it went with Janenne.

Favourite Finds

Spice Girls memorabilia

In the mid-1990s it was my personal opinion that the Spice Girls were the coolest people on the planet. I was six, or seven, and at my school the cool thing to do if you thought the Spice Girls were the coolest people on the planet was to collect Spice Girls memorabilia, particularly these little envelopes of photographs they sold at newsagents. You would store them in your own little photo album and trade with your friends to see how many different photographs you could collect. Anyway, mine were in a daggy little floral photo album that my Nanna gave me and I had a humble collection that I cherished. One day, I left my album on my desk for probably a millisecond and, when I turned back around, it was gone.

I was devastated. An older girl had taken it for herself and staunchly denied doing so, despite my feeble attempts at gaining justice by questioning her in person and almost begging the teachers to do a pat-down search. I've never gotten over my Spice Girls photo collection being stolen, until I found someone else's full Spice Girls photo collection in a thrift store and brought it home: and everything was right in the world again. I would have been, like, 22 when this happened, so it was a long road.

Stevie Nicks' *Hands Off!* self defence book

I would cite this book as one of my absolute 'Favourite Finds' of ALL TIME. This one, I stumbled across in the book section of Savers that I very regularly dissect (I think they're really sick of me in that place) and who did I see on the front cover but STEVIE NICKS doing a *Charlie's Angels* punch in a luscious-looking floral and flared jumpsuit. Jackpot! It's a book written in 1983 by a guy called Bob Jones who specialised in teaching women self-defence. Inside, there are demonstrations modelled by Nicks, such as how to scratch a guy in the face, how to kick a guy in the groin, and how to kick a guy in the chin with the chunky heel of your velvet boot. So useful.

'Stevie Nicks found *Hands Off!*'s mnemonic movements completely different from the movements of her stage performance. Her interest, besides self defence, was to include them in future stage presentation.' All I can say is that Lindsey Buckingham better watch out.

BOB JONES

Hands Off!

A unique new system of self defence against assault for the women of today

Stevie Nicks: lead singer of Fleetwood Mac

BAY BOOKS

HAPPY

LUNCHTIME

FROM

THE

SUPER JRS.

©DC
COMICS
INC.1979

Superhero Junior plastic lunch box

I found this in a thrift store: it's a 1970s plastic school kid's lunch box decorated with baby versions of superheroes like Wonder Woman and Batman. I use it to keep my coloured felt-tip pens in (among many other things) and I like to imagine all the knick-knacks and snacks and bugs that the child who owned this used to store in here on long hot school days.

Vintage 1960s pillboxes

These pillboxes are so tiny and beautiful. I love any kind of zodiac illustrations, as they're always so luminous and intricate. My star sign is Sagittarius, so this find seemed rather coincidental and I've treasured these on my bedside table for a long time. Okay, so they're not particularly practical. I don't have a myriad of pills to store in them and nothing else really fits. They're purely ornamental, which is dangerous. I have a penchant for purely ornamental things and, although these are tiny, they are contributing in large ways to the clutter in my room…

Firstly, a very large portion of my thanks goes to Tracey and Eugene Gilligan, my beloved Mum and Dad. Not only for their initial contribution of bringing me into this world, but for their encouragement and support that indeed knows no bounds. Mum, thank you for laughing at my jokes, for the mother–daughter days at Savers, for your unwavering faith in me, for rubbing off your exceptional taste on me and, yes, for coming up with the title of this book. Dad, thank you for shaping me into a hardworking individual, for your honest opinions that I truly value, and for believing in my ability even when I didn't believe in it myself. Thank you.

I'd also like to thank my two younger sisters, Eilish and Eden Gilligan.

Nanna Pam: you're a beacon of warmth, stability and strength. This has helped me on many occasions.

Nanna Helen, thank you for always being fiercely proud of me and for making Sunday night dinners compelling.

Thank you to every one of my aunties and uncles. A special mention to Aunty Therese: you have shaped me as a young women and artist in so many ways.

To my little cousins Chloe and Jordy, you are both sparkling, buoyant lights in my life.

Simon Walsh: my pragmatic, practical, and perfect partner in crime. You inspire and challenge me.

* * *

Everyone at Hardie Grant Books, but especially:

Fran Berry, for approaching me to make this book in the first place. It is a dream come true. Thank you so much for seeing that potential in me.

Meelee Soorkia, for your saintlike patience and your calm, considered and immensely valuable input.

Michelle Mackintosh, for tolerating my crazy creative processes and bringing this whole thing together into a book that looks both cohesive and beautiful.

Rich MacDonald for his slick photographic work.

* * *

My friends, especially Georgie Glanville, Jon Campbell, Brodie Lancaster, Therese Sheehy and Briallen Curtis.

Daine Singer. Thank you for taking on crazy ol' me. For your support above and beyond your duties as gallerist and friend.

All the *Rookie* mag staff, especially Tavi Gevinson, who, by taking me on at *Rookie*, has contributed largely to a lot of my dreams coming true.

Last, but certainly not least, my dog Soda.

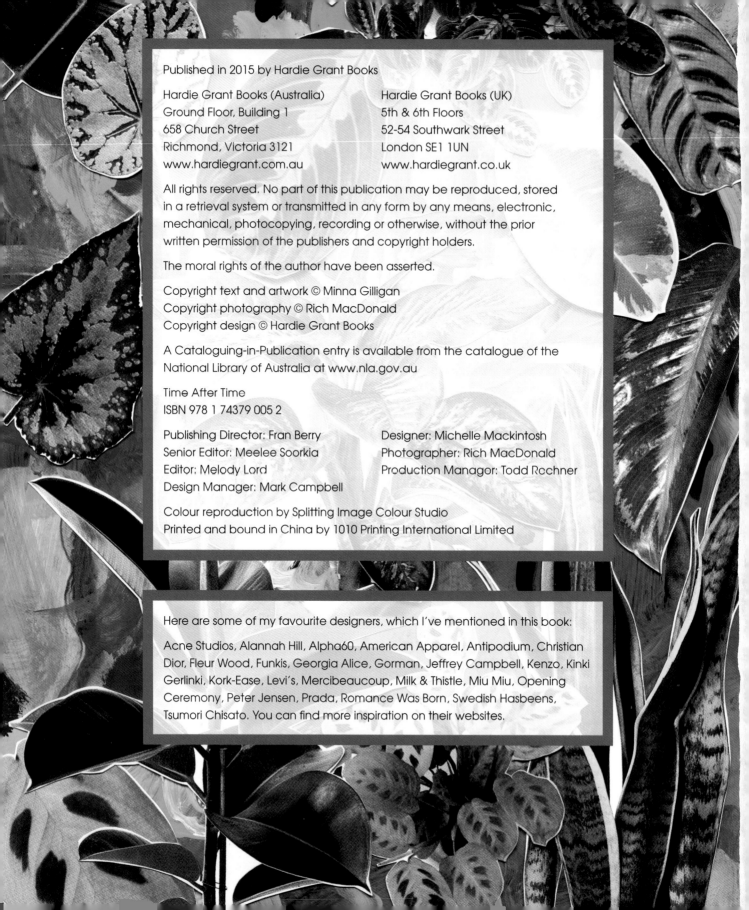

Published in 2015 by Hardie Grant Books

Hardie Grant Books (Australia)
Ground Floor, Building 1
658 Church Street
Richmond, Victoria 3121
www.hardiegrant.com.au

Hardie Grant Books (UK)
5th & 6th Floors
52-54 Southwark Street
London SE1 1UN
www.hardiegrant.co.uk

A Cataloguing-in-Publication entry is available from the catalogue of the National Library of Australia at www.nla.gov.au

Time After Time
ISBN 978 1 74379 005 2

Publishing Director: Fran Berry
Senior Editor: Meelee Soorkia
Editor: Melody Lord
Design Manager: Mark Campbell

Designer: Michelle Mackintosh
Photographer: Rich MacDonald
Production Manager: Todd Rechner

Colour reproduction by Splitting Image Colour Studio
Printed and bound in China by 1010 Printing International Limited

Here are some of my favourite designers, which I've mentioned in this book:

Acne Studios, Alannah Hill, Alpha60, American Apparel, Antipodium, Christian Dior, Fleur Wood, Funkis, Georgia Alice, Gorman, Jeffrey Campbell, Kenzo, Kinki Gerlinki, Kork-Ease, Levi's, Mercibeaucoup, Milk & Thistle, Miu Miu, Opening Ceremony, Peter Jensen, Prada, Romance Was Born, Swedish Hasbeens, Tsumori Chisato. You can find more inspiration on their websites.

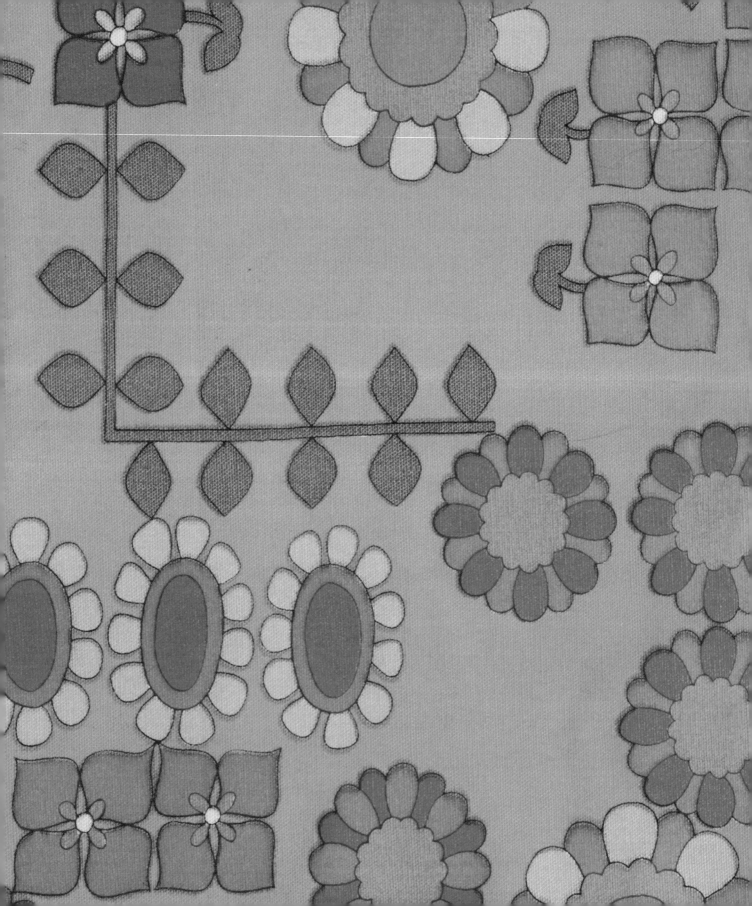